In the Right Light

THE PECKHAM CONNECTION

By Anna Green & Alice Malik

This is a first edition of
The Peckham Connection

by Anna Green & Alice Malik
Published in 2016 by In the Right Light

Graphic design by Ezra-Lloyd Jackson of DVLOP
Cover artwork by Jannette Parris
Preface by Keith Turpin

www.intherightlight.co.uk

ISBN : 978-0-9954919-0-8

The Peckham Connection

This book aims to tell a story about the diversity of enterprise in Peckham. We started by interviewing Jackie at Quick Print, a small, family-owned print company, then let our participants tell us where to go next. Our aim was to follow a trail which, we hoped, would describe a local business community. At the end of every interview we asked our participants where they thought we should go next and why. ntinued until we had included 50 businesses in this project.

The idea is to describe an economic community at a time when the spotlight is on change in Peckham . We have both lived the area ly for many years and have developed an interest in photographing people at work. We had seen and read a lot about new businesses in the area, but were also aware of the longevity of many others. So we were interested in the relationships between these, and wanted The Peckham Connection to be an accessible description of old and new enterprise in Peckham. This is a Peckham project, but it's relevance is broader. It's also a story about the constant flux of inner-city businesses.

We followed our trail between 2014 and 2016. On it, we visited businesses to the north, south, east and west of Peckham. Some were high-street shops and market stalls, some were more hidden studios and workshops. All the businesses included were independently owned - The Peckham Connection is a chain-free chain. We visited new businesses that had been open for less than six months and we visited a sixth-generation family business, Ayres the bakers.

Our chain evolved into a web, losing its linear nature. Some people gave us multiple referrals, other liks couldn't be made. The resulting network mirrors the organic nature of Peckham.

The businesses that we didn't manage to visit also have a story to tell: a patisserie had closed down; a steel fabricator had moved; a bar manager was always too busy; a traditional public house wasn't interested; a launderette manager was keen to take part but the owner wouldn't allow it. The narratives vary greatly, being grounded in many different individual experiences. We were interested, for example, in how a hairdresser became a dog-groomer, and how refugee from Afghanistan came to run a high-profile busines on a London high street; how a butler came to manage a hai salon, and how A E Wilson, the oldest business in Peckham, had survived since 1870 with hardly a change.

This is a story of diversity and cross-fertilisation. Owner employees and customers are European, African, Caribbean, Asian, American and Middle Eastern. Customers and owners o 10 don't share roots. For example, a vegetable stall on Ry Lane is owned by an Iraqi Kurd but caters for Jamaican customers. A West African textile shop is owned by an Afghani, and draws customers from far afield, some even sending fabric back home to be made up into clothes for weddings or special occasions.

Resilience, adaptation and independence are common threads these stories. Again and again we heard how businesses ha started up through a desire to not work for others, and by those seeking the quality of life they associated with working for themselves. For some it was because their choic were limited by not having UK qualifications. Stalls on Ry Lane were affordable and accessible to people just startin out in a way that most of London wasn't. At The General Store, the husband-and-wife team had chosen a way of life that allowed them to live and work together with low overheads.

With not working for others come long hours and risks. One of the key risks identified was that associated with renting property in an area of escalating prices. For some, property ownership provided long-term security; for others, 'good' landlords offered some stability. But many of these traders were very aware of their vulnerability to rising rents as Peckham gentrified.

The cyclical nature of business was apparent. Review, the bookshop, was seen as the beginning of a new wave of local business when it opened in 2005; Maestro Records had sent us there for that reason. But 10 years on, Review is now an established elder. Akbar, the owner of Khan's commented on how specialist shops close down in times of recession, leading his shop to fill these gaps in the market by expanding its stock. Ayres the Baker survived and prospered through a recession by closing shops. In many different ways these entrepreneurs of Peckham describe the ebb and flow of local businesses. Each wave leaves Peckham with something new.

Barry, our local historian, himself embodies this dynamism, longevity and passion for Peckham. Barry ran Barry's Autos on Blenheim Grove, where he has lived, for many years. We met him at Barry's Café, his retirement business. A nice touch that Barry was late meeting us because he was giving some panel-beating tips to the knife-makers at the foundry: a new business was learning from the experience of the old. Such integration is also illustrated in our chain, which links new and established enterprise. James at Peckham Refreshment Rooms described how being connected to the area is vital to his business.

In conclusion, The Peckham Connection offers a colourful description of an enterprising, hardworking, diverse and dynamic business community. Each story generated is a jewel in itself, highlighting the huge variety of career paths available, and offering a window into a bigger and richer world – a Peckham experiment of which they are each a part.

Anna Green & Alice Malik

May 2016

Cappuccino, cassava, carrots and cocktails

This celebration of the diversity and creativity of small-scale independent shops and enterprises currently flourishing in Peckham provides a fascinating insight into a long and varied history of shopping in the area.

It is difficult to appreciate through our contemporary understanding of what constitutes the experience of shopping (going to the West End; huge shopping malls and retail parks both in and out of town; and, of course, on-line) how developed, locally distinctive and sophisticated were south-east London's high streets. Peckham's crowning glories were opulent and architecturally distinctive department stores modeled on West End prototypes. Clapham, Streatham, Brixton and Peckham, with its ornately Italianate Jones & Higgins building (at the gateway to Rye Lane), were all immensely busy and popular major retail centres and supported a variety of well-known names until the early 1980s.

What followed in the ensuing decades? A shift in demographics and populations, changing shopping behaviours and local consumer needs saw a complete change as branded, internalised and formally appointed retail space gave way to a far looser, often externalised and smaller scale re-arrangement of the existing structures and spaces, creating a huge street market spilling onto the pavements, vibrant in colour, textures and smells, from fresh fish and traditional fruit'n'veg to textiles.

Nostalgia for familiar landmarks and perhaps a certain regret held sway as some commodities once locally sourced required a longer journey, but within the past decade Peckham has been in the vanguard of a shopping counterculture that has reinvigorated many local neighbourhoods as a reaction to monolithic and homogenising retail parks and malls.

The businesses whose individuality and bespoke character are captured so effectively in these photographs and accompanying text have seized the creative and entrepreneurial zeitgeist that has become Peckham's distinctive trademark in the last decade or so. Coffee shops, pop-up bars and restaurants and almost daily local additions to the high street bear testimony to our neighbourhood's current cultural and artistic status.

CAPPACINO, CASSAVA, CARROTS AND COCTAILS

But what of the future? Some see diversity and increasing choice, but others see rapidly escalating gentrification and the squeezing of precisely those small-scale enterprises that have become well established since the 1980s and 1990s, but which preceded the hip and trendy Peckham that has so recently, and perhaps surprisingly, sprung up around us.

Cappuccino, cassava, carrots and cocktails currently all jostle for our attention, but change is afoot. Major development plans are coming at both town and borough level: around the station, the market square, the Aylesham Centre. Enterprises tucked in arcades and side streets and under arches need to be safeguarded or sensitively relocated. We have to ensure that everything this book celebrates is not marginalized or superseded by bland uniformity, as has happened in so many other areas of London.

The Peckham Connection has wonderfully captured the present moment in Peckham's long love affair with shopping, a moment we all need to seize and safeguard for the future.

Keith Turpin local historian

QUICK PRINT

Jackie at Quick Print

The first business we approached was Quick Print, as we already knew Jackie. What a great starting point this was for our chain: an established family enterprise with its origins in Peckham from the days the neighbourhood was known as Print Village, as there were so many printers in the area.

Jackie's father, Victor, her husband Raymond, and Loretta, her mother, work together. Victor set up the business more than 50 years ago from a garage on Lyndhurst Way. He had trained at the London College of Printing before it moved to Elephant and Castle. The business then was largely typesetting using a hand press:

"We used an Adana press which is still here in the back of the shop, and then moved to a treadle."

After a few years they moved to where they are now. Victor and Loretta lived above the business. In those days print companies dominated the area.

"We were always the smallest, and now we are the sole survivor. They all did different printing; our service was what made us survive. Quick Print was the first business to advertise same-day printing; people even came from abroad for our quick service. We never said no."

When asked where they would like to be in 10 years, Jackie's answer was clear.

"We like being here as we live locally. For 15 years we even ran a successful plumbing business from the same premises but we always came back to printing. In 10 years, we will still be here. With paper you can't go wrong."

Jackie suggested that we start off our chain by visiting Maestro Records, Callow Locksmiths, Dog about Town and Thames Gallery, because they had all been in the area for at least 20 years.

MAESTRO RECORDS

Maestro Michael

Michael of Maestro Records started his business more than 20 years ago.

Originally he had a Saturday job at Bam Records, which had branches in Peckham, Petticoat Lane and Walthamstow. His own record business started in Peckham covered market and then moved to 61 Rye Lane and only moved around the corner a month before we met him in 2014.

The business has changed a little since he started. There were no computers to begin with: everything was done in person or over the phone. Some things about the music business haven't changed as much as you'd imagine. For example, Michael is now selling vinyl again.

What Michael likes about being in Peckham is serving the community. He has many regular customers, some of whom have been coming back since he opened his business. On the day we visited the shop there was a customer there who had been a regular for more than 20 years.

Maestro customers can buy a wide range of music, including reggae, ska, hip-hop, r'n'b, gospel, and soca, as well as tickets to music events happening across London.

Michael does not live in Peckham any more, but commutes from Stanmore in north-west London. When asked how that came to be, he said that when he put a ring on his wife's finger, she refused to live in south-east London.

We asked him where he'd like to be in 10 years.

"Right here with my customers," he said.

And where would he like us to go next?

Michael sent us to Review on Bellenden Road, not because he was a customer but because

“it was the first shop that showed a sign that Peckham was changing.”

Object Lessons
R E V I E W

Roz of Review

Review, the bookshop on Bellenden Road, opened in 2005. Roz landed there after having lived in the area for a long time, since the days when it was known locally as the British Rail Devastation Area. Roz said there had been a lot of cynicism when she first opened, with people saying there was no call for books around here. But they were proved wrong.

Review is a quirky independent bookshop with an interest in design and creativity, and a love of dogs! The shop counter reflects the attention to detail and also the skills of Roy, Roz's partner, a set designer and cabinet-maker. Roz now lives in Ireland with Gus the lurcher, who never likes to be out of his owners' sight, and was for many years a feature of the bookshop, a local character. Roz usually comes back to Peckham for a few days each month.

Roz's attitude is very much that you never know what the future holds. Review is now managed over a distance of 578km, in a very modern way. There's no broadband where Roz lives in Ireland so she has had satellite internet installed, with which she makes the book orders and manages the accounts from Tipperary.

Roz said that she would have liked to have sent us to Maria of Fenton Walsh, as both shops had set up at the same time and shared many similar experiences. But sadly, this boutique closed down recently - a marker of the precariousness of small independent businesses.

Roz also suggested Ben at Bar Story, so we went to see him several times, but he was always too busy to talk. And she suggested Andy, a steel fabricator in Blenheim Arches, who had moved away by the time we went to visit him.

C A L L O W L O C K S M I T H S

Team Scott at the lock shop

Tom and Scott were at the locksmiths when we arrived. Tom was serving a customer who needed to replace a door lock and Scott was stock-taking. Jack returned from a job soon after we arrived. Just as we were leaving, the guv'nor, Scott Callow, turned up. The uniformed four felt like family and so it was pleasing to learn that although not family by birth, Tom and Jack were indeed related by marriage.

Scott, the boss, set the business up in a small shop at number 98 Lordship Lane in 1988. Soon afterwards they moved across the road to larger premises, and then in September 2013 to Melbourne Grove. Scott the younger has been with the firm for 16 years, Jack for 12 and Tom nearly five years. Their business, they say, is **"everything and anything to do with locks"**. When we asked if the work had changed over the years, we were told: **"It is pretty much the same, but there are more cases of people being locked out of their own homes, mostly women!"** Perhaps we can translate this positively as meaning that there are now more independent women living in the area.

In 10 years Scott, Jack and Tom hope to jointly own the business when Scott retires and sell up.

Not bad at 54 years.

Being a Peckham boy, Tom sent us on to Manze's pie and mash shop, where he ate as a lad. So did Scott jnr, whose nan and nandad, he said, lived practically opposite.

Scott the boss then added Ayres, the bakery on Evelina Road.

M A N Z E

Mr Manze

Manze's opened in Peckham in 1927, the fifth and last of the Manze shops. The tiled interior is truly vintage, a style that suits both old and new Peckham. The shop is well documented: Just last week Heston Blumenthal was here for TV.

We met with Graham, one of three brothers (Graham, Geoff and Richard) running Manze's shops in Tower Bridge, Peckham and Sutton. Graham does not portray himself as a Peckham man. When asked about other businesses in the area, Graham said, with a twinkle, that he would not know where to send us. He had not been down Rye Lane for years – he explained that he just turns left out of the shop door to where he parks his car and then drives straight home to Croydon.

Customers in Peckham are mainly local compared to those at Tower Bridge, where they see mostly tourists. The core of the shop is unchanged. Manze still serves the same food, using the same recipes, as it did in the 1890s: pie, mash, liquor and eels, only nowadays, as Graham said, the prices have gone up from the original penny a pie.

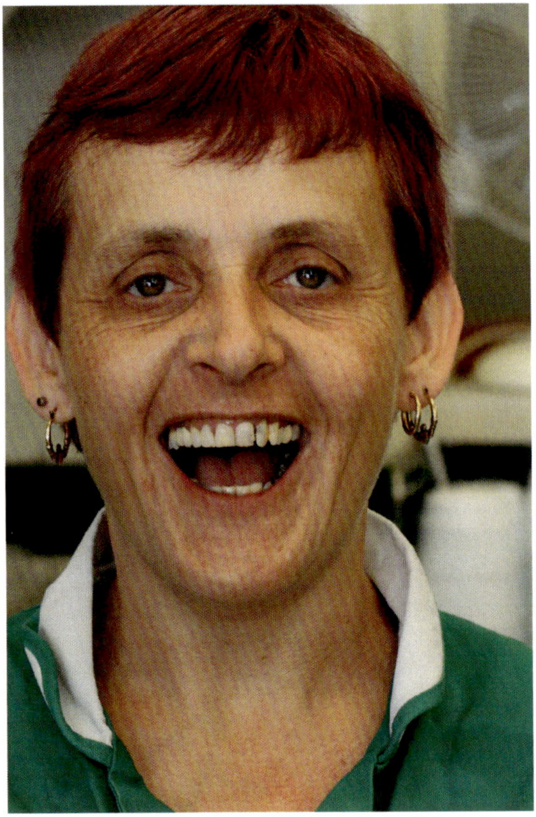

This family business may be at the end of the line. Graham doesn't have any sons to take it over and feels that his daughter, who has spent four years at university, should do something else and not, to his mind, waste her education. He sees the business as being very much a man's job. Perhaps his daughter would disagree?

After some thought Graham suggested we went up the road to Whitten Timber, another historic Peckham institution.

A Y R E S
SHIPTON MILL
SHIPTON MILL

Ayres the baker

We spent half an hour in Ayres bakery before Vincent arrived; in this time we saw a steady stream of customers coming in for bread, cakes and coffee. Five people made up the Ayres team and the atmosphere was busy and cheerful. Vincent had recently returned from his holiday home in Spain. He was looking tanned and relaxed. We went upstairs to his office.

Ayres is a family business. It was originally set up by Fred Ayre, Vincent's father, in 1955. Vincent took over in the early 1980s. He is the sixth-generation baker in the family. His work, he said, is hard – not just being a baker, but running a business. He had friends who earned three times as much as he did, but he acknowledged that he valued his freedom and independence. He also appreciated that he had had good support and advice throughout his career.

Vince's secret confession was that his family only eats supermarket pitta bread. Pitta is a recipe that Ayres has not cracked!

Where to next?

The Dish and the Spoon in Cheltenham Road, a great new business.

W H I T T E N
T I M B E R

James Whitten talks timber

James Whitten is the great-great-grandson of William Henry Whitten who started Whitten & Sons in 1919, selling firewood reclaimed from WWI ammunition boxes. The business expanded to become a large family timber merchant, distributing timber across London by way of the Surrey Docks canal network link to Peckham.

We met James in the summer of 2014 just after he had written a history of the business, Something Very Extraordinary: The Whitten Timber Story, and was curating an exhibition at Peckham Platform. The story of Whitten characterises both the endurance and transformations of businesses in Peckham, and is well worth reading.

James is not only a family historian but also an artist. We met with him at the counter of the yard. He shares the business with his older brother John and his father Robert, who is now semi-retired. We spoke to James upstairs in his office, which is also a gallery of his own paintings and those he has collected, many from local artists. James, unsurprisingly, has a penchant for collecting paintings on and of wood. We didn't speak with John, the older brother, but learnt that he was also a passionate hobbyist, a fisherman.

At Whitten's you can feel the legacy of a war-time business – nothing goes to waste. Not many timber merchants have a bits-and-pieces bucket selling odd offcuts for just 50p.

Where to next? James sent us just around the corner, to Peckham's oldest business, A E Wilson.

THE DISH & THE SPOON

Shona's Dish & Spoon

Vince from Ayres Bakery sent us to the Dish & the Spoon on a residential road south-east of Peckham Rye. He is a regular, appreciating the quality offerings of Dark Fluid Coffee, which is roasted in nearby Grove Park.

Shona's business has had a rocky start. She was forced to close down for several months after a burst pipe under the floor caused a flood. When we met, in March 2015, the final fittings were being made, and a couple of customers popped in to welcome her back.

The Dish & the Spoon is a child-friendly space. Parents with buggies are encouraged in and made to feel relaxed and welcomed. Shona used to work in marketing, so knew how to do her research; in her first year of business she won a best toddler-friendly-café award.

Shona lives in Forest Hill now, but the idea for the café came when she lived just around the corner and was aware that there was nothing offered locally in the daytime. The building was available and Shona took the opportunity of a 15-year lease. But she's still seeking out that elusive family-friendly work-life balance. She has a five-year-old son and is pregnant again.

Shona has lots of ideas and projects, with more to come; the café has a flexible space on offer to community groups and for private functions on evenings and weekends. She is open to ideas and networking mainly through word-of-mouth and social media.

Where to next? Shona suggested Rat Race Cycles – another new business that is child-friendly. Rusby Cycles had already sent us there, so it was a double connection.

A E WILSON

Steve at Wilson's

It took us a while to pin down Steve, the owner of Wilson's; we were determined to see him, as we knew that Wilson's was the oldest business in Peckham, running since 1870. Steve has taken over from the third generation of Wilson's; he's experienced in the bike trade, and local. He left Peckham Manor School at 16 to work for a West End bicycle company, then within six months he was promoted to area manager. He was bike-crazy when he was young, and spoke about designing the successful Muddy Fox Courier bike.

Lee works alongside Steve. In the time we were there he was dealing with customers and fixing bikes. Lee is interested in the history of Wilson's. He pointed out the original glass-and-steel counter and the very solid bike-stand, still being used on a daily basis for repairs.

Steve says there have been many changes in the area and many new bike shops have opened. There is room in the market though, as there are so many more bikes. The biggest change here is that there are many more expensive bikes, but the repair and maintenance of these are the same.

Steve no longer lives in Peckham, but commutes to work: **"When you grow up somewhere and work there too, you really want to try somewhere else, and Peckham has become very expensive."**

Where would he like to be in 10 years? **"On a sunny island,"** was Steve's first and probably honest answer before he corrected himself to saying, **"Here of course."** Steve is confident that the business will still be here - even the rental of the building he saw as being secure.

Where to next, Steve?

“Peckham Spares, not bikes but cars.”

PECKHAM SPARES

Harry and Mandy

"Hello, Peckham!" Harry said into the telephone as we entered Peckham Spares.

Harry and Mandy are a brother-and-sister team. They ran around the shop when they were children, and now they are running the place. Their dad bought Peckham Spares, both the business and the building, in partnership with their uncle, at an auction 35 years ago: their uncle was a mechanic and knew his trade.

Mandy has been working in the shop for five years and in that time has learnt a lot about cars. Harry, on the other hand, is a lifer. He worked here as a child on weekends and diuring school holidays, and has now been full-time for 18 years. The family lives in Harrow.

So why Peckham?

Because it was affordable and available at the time they invested in the business. And to a family of car-lovers, perhaps the distance was not daunting.

As a hobby, Mandy likes to draw and paint, often cars. She was interested to learn that James, just across the road at Whitten Timber, shares her interest in art and also works with his brother.

In 10 years Harry would like to be a millionaire. He corrects himself; nowadays he'd need to be a billionaire! Anything related to the car trade is going to struggle, he feels, as restrictions imposed on the disposal of oil make life difficult for London garages.

Where to next? Katies
chicken shop next door.

KATIES

Omer not Katie

Katies was bought by Omer in 1994, and is one of Peckham's original chicken shops. It was a going concern when Omer bought it. Katie was the wife of the previous owner who, like Omer, was from Turkey, but she was tired of the long hours her husband worked and made him sell up.

Omer had been working for Transport for London for nearly 10 years when he decided that he had had enough and wanted to run his own business. He heard about Katies through a friend, then bought the premises and took on a lease with Southwark council; and that's how he ended up in Peckham.

Running Katies has many challenges. There were only three chicken shops in the whole of Peckham in 1994; now there are at least 23, maybe more. A new shop has just opened around the corner with much lower prices. The chicken market is so competitive that it is impossible to make a profit and to look after staff and premises properly. Katies employs three staff, and Omer is there most of the time. Eighty per cent of customers are regulars but even regulars shop elsewhere if the prices are lower. Omer feels that the council should do more to prevent too much competition.

The parade of shops by Peckham Library is like a family, slightly separate from the busier Rye Lane and Queens Road. Omer has expanded and also runs Katies Kebab Shop across the road. It is a friendly business community, but it is tough. Omer does recognise that there have been some improvements: for example, the streets are now safer and there is less crime. There have been big changes with the redevelopment of the North Peckham Estate and the building of Peckham Pulse across the road.

Where would Omer like to be in 10 years? **"Far, far, away from catering, on a beach."**

Our impression was that Omer was in a hard end of the market to run a business from, and that the customers could be thankless.

We did not ask Omer where to go next as we had already reached our target of 50 businesses.

DOG ABOUT TOWN

Stephen about town

Stephen is the third owner of Dog About Town and has run the business for nearly 20 years.

He used to live above the shop, but now commutes from Clapham. Stephen talked to us while skillfully handling a fox terrier. The dog looked happy to us but Stephen said he could turn at the pull of a knot. We were told that dog-grooming was harder than being a hairdresser. He would know as his career path was from human to dog grooming. Nicola his trainee has always wanted to work with animals. She had thought about becoming a vet but after having completed work experience here persuaded her nan, who lived nearby, to ask on her behalf for a job.

How has the business changed?

When Stephen took it over it was very, very pink, pink walls, pink pens and even pink poodles. It had to be got rid of, said the man in the pink shirt! Another change has been Stephen's breed specialism. He has moved from poodles, to bichons, to griffons for his pets, which he shows, and he also works as a judge. There was an impressive array of rosettes on the wall. Customers showing dogs would come many miles for a pre-competition groom; one bichon travels from Edinburgh.

The best thing about Stephen's work is his relationships with the dogs, and through the dogs, their owners. Clients tend to be regular, sometimes coming every six weeks. This makes it hard when doggy-customers die. The canine-client relationship is inevitably shortened by a dog's lifespan; some owners then disappear, whilst others reappear with a new dog.

In 10 years Steve hopes to have relocated to his hometown, Portsmouth, where he has already set up a dog parlour. All hope this business will continue in Nicola's safe hands.

Stephen and Nicola recommended that we next visit Flock & Herd, the butcher across the road. We felt that would also have been a popular choice amongst the dogs.

FLOCK & HERD

FLOCK × HERD
Butchery
FLOCK × HERD
Butchery
FLOCK × HERD
Butchery

Charlie the butcher

Charlie was about to set off on his deliveries to local restaurants when we arrived. The rest of the team was busy preparing meat and making sausages, as well as serving customers. The shop has four full-time workers plus several part-timers.
The impression is of a group of skilled mates working together.

Flock & Herd opened in September 2012. Charlie grew up in Greenwich, but hung out a lot with his cousin, Sam, who lived around the corner from Bellenden Road.

This was very much his community, which he defined more widely as south-east London:

"I like south-east London in general for its mix of people and its green spaces."

Charlie loves the variety of shops on Bellenden Road, with no chains, as well as the wide pavements and the curve of the street and, of course, his customers. Charlie gave a detailed description of the street – visuals are clearly important to him. You can see this not only from how from how he dresses, but also from the attention to detail in the shop design. He really feels part of the community and loves it when his customers come to his shop and not only know him, but also know each other. His customers, he says, are **"everyone and anyone, from the lollipop lady who comes here for chicken carcasses, to the dude from the IT Crowd. I am as happy if they spend 50p or £50."**

When asked where he would like to be in 10 years, Charlie grinned and said **“on a cruise ship in Barbados”**. This was a joke: in fact, he couldn’t think of anything worse. In reality Charlie would like to **“be here, and with a second shop”**. Perhaps the first chain on the street!

Where to next, Charlie?

Hugh at Peckham Print Studio, Peckham Refreshment Rooms on Blenheim Grove, and Matt in Petitou. Charlie likes it there - it used to be a butcher's shop as well.

P E C K H A M
R E F R E S H M E N T
R O O M S

Refreshments with James

We met with James at Peckham Refreshment Rooms, where he is joint owner. This vibrant bar-restaurant was set up in 2012. Both partners had lived in the area for many years. James's background is as a chef and restaurateur, and Sven, his partner 'was a director in arts and entertainment. Both juggle at least two jobs, enabling them to self-finance.

Connectivity to the area is a vital element of their business. James believes the success of this business is unique to this community and could not be replicated. The raw materials of the business are all sourced from a five-mile radius: fixtures and fittings are all fashioned by local designers.

James emphasises that a business needs to invest in people. Customers and staff must feel empowered and willing to say what is right and not right for them. James does not believe in the simplicity of the notion of gentrification of the area: his experience is of change and diversity. A diversity which enriches the area and is inclusive; a cross-fertilisation of different communities.

Seventy per cent of the restaurant's customers are women. This is because women respond to the safe environment and because the Refreshment Rooms provides what women want, such as small glasses of wine and small sharing dishes of charcuterie. **"Customers' needs are eclectic. Last night one table spent more than £100 on food and wine, next to another just having one drink. The Refreshment Rooms caters for all."**

In 10 years James would like to still be here. **"A good business is like a tree that grows slowly but is very tough."**

When asked where we should go next James suggested Kahn's on Rye Lane, which supplies herbs and spices to the Refreshment Rooms.

P E T I T O U

Matt's venture

One appeal of this coffee shop to Charlie the butcher was that it had originally been a butcher shop. Matt showed us a ledger of meat orders dating back to the 1930s. Today Flock & Herd, just around the corner, supplies Petitou with meat.

Matt grew up in Brockley but his parents and grandparents had lived in Peckham. Although local, he travelled from the Caribbean to open Petitou, with his partner Clare, inspired by a café in the Caribbean island of Saint Martin called Top Carrot where the food and atmosphere were both good. Clare's sister spotted the potential of the lovely building, derelict but beautiful with its large window and impressive tree outside. The building was a significant deciding factor in starting this new business, and Petitou opened in 2003.

Petitou, Matt says, has not changed in itself over the years but it has become a lot busier **"and a lot more serious".** He's happy and settled in the area with his family. But he is an adventurer, and so not surprisingly was not able to say whether or not he would still be here in 10 years' time.

Where to next?
Down the road
to his local,
The Montpelier.

KHAN'S BARGAINS

Akbar Khan's bargains

James send us to Khan's, supplier of spices to his restaurant and one of the best-known shops in Peckham. Khan's has the largest shopfront on Rye Lane in what was once Holdron's, the sophisticated department store, which closed down in 1949. Akbar Khan is now working on the restoration of this Art Deco building.

Akbar started his business in Peckham in 1999. He came to London from Kabul, where his family had run a wholesale business, after political unrest in Afghanistan and the disappearance of his father – he chose Peckham because he already had a cousin here. With no qualifications and only limited English, Akbar started a tabletop stall in front of what is now his shop. At that time there were many independent stalls within and outside this beautiful art deco building. When it was sold in 2003, the new owner wanted a single trader. Akbar took the opportunity, and the risk.

Khan's is now an enormous emporium selling fruit and vegetables, spices, groceries, homeware and kitchenware, cosmetics, stationery, DIY goods and more. What is striking is how much stock and choice there is within each department. Akbar takes pride in choice and explains that he is not becoming rich, but working hard to earn a living.

Akbar set up his business without borrowing any money; instead, he is given credit by his regular suppliers. This model has continued to work well. Many shops were forced to close in Peckham during the recession of the late 1990s and Khan's filled some of the gaps. For example, the electrical section expanded when the electrical shop on Rye Lane closed, and when Woolworths closed in 2009, Khan's stepped up to the mark and supplies many of the goods once found in Woolworths.

In 10 years Akbar would like to be where he is now, but expanded, and with the building restored to its former glory.

THE MONTPELIER

Neil at the Mont

We met Neil at the Montpelier at the end of what had been one of the busiest, and hottest, lunchtimes of the year so far. Glasses of chilled water all round. Neil set up the Parched Pubs Company eight years ago with three friends. All are equal partners and they are running strong. The Montpelier, their fourth pub, was opened in 2010 - they also manage two pubs in the Borough and one in Streatham. The Montpelier was targeted for being in an exciting and fast-changing area and so far, and has exceeded expectations.

The Victoria, futher up Choumert Road, opened in the same week. Both are thriving.

Neil lives and works on Choumert Road and says that he lives and breathes the street. He clearly also loves the traditional idea of the local, and the history of the area.

He describes the pub as a multi-layered business, not only a pub but also a restaurant, cinema and coffee shop. To compete, it has to be good at each of these, with food as a growing focus. Neil clearly gets a buzz from his work, but it is difficult in terms of hours and energy. The Montpelier has 15 staff, many of whom live in accommodation above the pub.

In 10 years Neil hopes to be here still, but that depends on the landlord. He would also like to start a restaurant in the area.

Neil suggested that our next connection should be John Payne, the local builder, whom we never managed to meet. But as we left the pub we were approached by Andrew and sent to Otherwise the tailors in Bellended Road.

O T H E R W I S E

Otherwise Andrew

Andrew brought us from the Montpelier to Otherwise Design as part of his quest to promote the incredible yet hidden work of Christopher and Lera. Andrew's enthusiasm was both infectious and justified.

Christopher, we were told, is an immensely skilled pattern designer, maker and manufacturer for the fashion industry. He'd taken on Andrew just six weeks ago as an apprentice bespoke tailor, and Andrew has been blown away by the way Christopher invests in and trusts people. Andrew's story is itself interesting but he really wanted us to hear about Christopher and Lera who had worked together for many years.

Christopher trained 50 years ago at Central Saint Martins and then at the London School of Fashion. In his early days in Trinidad, he gained a reputation for clothes alterations. When high-waisted double-pleated trousers were the fashion he made them for his friends, and when they were no longer in fashion, he altered them. He still provides this service for people who come to him.

While we were there, Alfred, a regular, arrived with a pile of material and a vision, leaving it with Christopher to make of it what he would. Samples were being considered and reworked. Christopher was recreating the pattern for a beautifully tailored colonial jacket, which he was planning to produce in a range of fabrics, many of them with traditional African patterns.

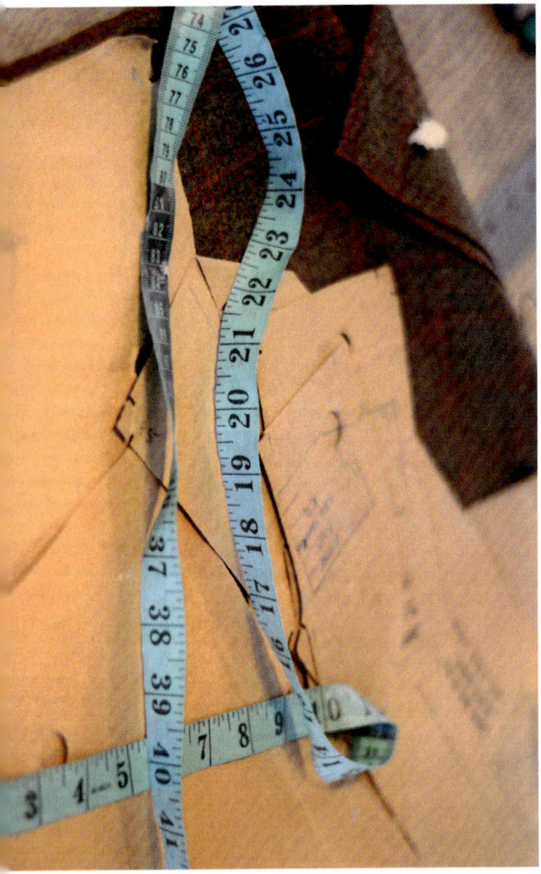

For Andrew, knowing where he'd like to be in 10 years is easy – he wanted to have the skills to create as Christopher does. **"I am not concerned with the money but with quality of life."** And he would like Christopher and Lera to be recognized for their brilliance and to be billionaires: **"They deserve it."**

Andrew sent us on to the new patisserie on Choumert Road. Sadly, by the time we got there, the business had moved on.

PECKHAM PRINT STUDIO

Printing in Peckham

Perhaps Peckham is still Print Village. We are now at a print studio, recently set up by Hugh and Nathan, fresh from the London College of Communication. Peckham Print Studio is a screen-printing studio offering open-access membership, workshops and a commercial printing service. Hugh and Nathan graduated in 2011, worked in Bermondsey for a short while and then were offered this space and went for it.

"There are not many places for people to print. We wanted to print and to give others the opportunity to print."

Nathan and Hugh are enthusiastic and young and, as yet, our youngest business. They already employ a studio manager, Tom, to focus on generating business through memberships, freeing up time for commercial work and workshops. They both also work in pubs in the evenings. Their business is equipment-heavy, and their equipment is on offer to everyone and anyone who would like to learn to screen-print. They recently made a portable printer for events.

Nathan and Hugh both love thei immediate surroundings – the galler upstairs, coffee shops, newsagents **"There is a wealth of busines and we all look out for each other It's not Loadsamoney but it is nice rich environment."** There i a lot happening in the area, wit many plans for re-development. I is clear that they hope to be wher they are now in 10 years, withi this already vibrant community

Hugh's mum, who is now retired used to work round the corne at Bellenden Primary School She particularly likes a cha with Charlie the butcher

H

Lois sells hand
working in the

The one thi
was that she
started train
"midwife crisi
for more than
premises bec
six months

Helen has su
with beaut
She describes
being a curato
**"But like bein
eat everythi
as tempting as**
is enthusiast
but with a
of pragmatis
her shop and
pays herself
and works ve
She's open s
but isn't
established t

Helen clearly h
and successful
she describes
Choumert Squa
a collector c
when a ne
Helen loves

Hugh and Nathan sent us on to Jamie of JailMake, just off Peckham Rye, who is a designer, and to Helen at Lois in Choumert Road.

Looking ahead 10 years, she said, was too much. When we met in 2014, her challenge was to stay open for the sales that Christmas and to end the year on a profit.

Lois suggested that after visiting her shop, we went next door to Café Viva. Like Hugh and Nathan at the Peckham Print Studio, she also suggested Jamie at JailMake.

Viva le Café

Café Viva is a small cafe serving coffee and food on Choumert Road in the heart of Peckham. Lily opened up in March 2012. She has worked in many cafes and restaurants, in the kitchens and as a waitress, since the age of 16.

Lily settled in south-east London when she was a textiles student at Goldsmiths. She spotted her site when an African café shut down and was able to invest a small inheritance. Lily lives in a flat above Lois's next door and so practically lives above her business. She has always had roots in the area; she was born in East Dulwich Hospital.

Lily likes where she is, between Rye Lane and Bellenden Road. She likened it to being on the edge of two sides of Peckham, a melting pot. Her customers too are a real mix of students, locals from very immediate streets, young parents with their newborns and, at weekends, more and more Peckham day-trippers, which would have been unimaginable even two years ago.

Lily feels there has been little change in Café Viva since opening but there are big changes to come for her, as she is now eight months pregnant. Living so close to her work will then be a huge benefit to her. Lily has nine staff, all working part-time, who will enable her to keep running her business. When asked where she would like to be in 10 years, Lily says she is not sure.

Lily sent us on to Rose Household & Party Stuffs a few doors down from her café, and also to Paula at Laundromat on Bellenden Road.

R O S E ' S

Rose Household & Party Stuffs

Rose opened her shop in 2003. Before that, she and her husband had been working night shifts from 6pm until 6am. That had suited them well while they were on their own, but their daughters were born in 1998 and 2000 and Rose wanted to be able to look after her children, and felt she could best do that by running her own business.

In those early days, Rose said, the shop had been busier. There was less competition from other shops, especially the more prominent pound shops. Rose relies on the loyalty of regular customers – we were in the shop for 30 minutes and every couple of minutes someone popped in. All were greeted in a familial way.

Church is an important feature of Rose's community and relationships. She is a member of the Reality of Grace Ministry. Rose said it is really important in her life, and that the Bible says we shouldn't forfeit the assembly of one another, but value the comfort and support that people offer. These ideals are apparent in Rose's kind manner and in her real efforts to introduce us to more businesses. Rose was really willing to help us with our project.

In 10 years Rose would still like to run this business but she would like it to be bigger and to specialise more in party goods. If not right here she would like to be open in a more lucrative area, where people would think less about their spending. Costs are going up, including rents, she said, and her customers are always trying to bring the prices down, and that is hard.

Rose sent us across the road to Lollypop Couture, another West African business.

LOLLYPOP

Lollypop

Rose introduced us to Lollypop, who we interviewed there and then. Lollypop, we learn, is both a fashion designer and recording artist. Lollypop is the shop, the man and the brand. Lollypop adopted his brand name as his own. A key part of his business is making one-off clothes for musical stars all over the world. Lollypop houses six lines including his very first, **"Pop."**

Lollypop started up six years ago in Peckham; in 10 years he wants to be here still but even more successful, and bigger. Lollypop is on a mission not just for himself but also to be a role model to young people, to show that there are alternatives to gangsta street life. **"You can make it today and be a good example. I want to make it here for Peckham and the community."** Lollypop is proud to work with everyone in his diverse community, and across many musical genres including rap, afro beat, urban beat and reggae.

The crossover between music and fashion is very big business; today for example we have rap billionaire Dr Dre who made big money through fashion headphones (Dr Dre Beats). We spoke outside on the street but entering the shop was like stepping into a world of showbiz glamour. The sparkle of Lollypop's shoes, clothes and hats is spectacular.

The shop is a social hub. Outside on the street, networking is face-to-face, where Lollypop is hanging out with his artists, DJs and friends. We met his friend Mantana who had just produced a single with Lollypop.

Where next? To Iopi who runs the recording studio across the road - sadly - we never caught him at the right time.

JAIL
MAKE

Jamie and the makers

JailMake is a 3D design and fabrication workshop tucked away on a small industrial site close to Peckham Rye.

The core team is made up of Jamie, who is the director, a studio manager and two juniors. Their office is at the front of the building, and there's a workshop bursting with machines and materials at the rear. Practically everything in the building is self-made. Jamie was directing a big clear-up as the team was in the process of expanding into a space next door, as well as clearing space for a Christmas banquet.

Jamie studied design at Goldsmiths. From there, he was headhunted by a design studio in Spain where he worked for five months before returning to London with his then-partner to set up their design studios. Where the name JailMake came from is top secret! The business has been built up over seven years with no loans, all self-funded. The team moved here from Deptford and love it.

Jamie lives and works in SE15, which he feels is as near to central London as he could be with this type of property. It is a nice community to be in, but Jamie stresses that he also has his own community within JailMake. He has local clients, particularly artists, as well as clients from further afield.

Jamie is excited and passionate about making things, and has a particular interest in engineering and robotics. He is doing what he wants to be doing.

In 10 years Jamie would like to have expanded but not too much. JailMake is already taking on the space next door; it would be good also to have an office upstairs. Workwise, though, he would like just to be doing the same, but cherry-picking his jobs for the ones that involve more complexity.

Where to next? Jamie sent us to his stablemate Oli at Tableflip.

TABLEFLIP

TOPICS FROM MATHEMATICS
COMPUTERS
Cambridge University Press
SHIRTS · COLLARS · PYJAMAS

Tableflip Oli

Oli shares his front office with Jamie. Tableflip occupies two large desks surrounded by techie, creative and philosophical materials. Whilst we were there the team consisted of just Oli and a young programmer. As with many of our SE15 entrepreneurs, Oli is a graduate of Goldsmiths.

Tableflip was founded by two freelance web designers who made their money working for large organisations, but wanted to free users to be able to control their own systems. Their interest is in open-source code, helping individuals to develop their own code and applications. To do this Tableflip facilitates community events under the aegis of Meteor, Nodeschool London and NodeBots, applying the same model to robotics, as well as teaching code-making (and breaking) to children in local schools.

Oli explained that he dedicates 50 per cent of his time to paid clients and 50 per cent to his open-source community work. He loves being based in SE15, away from the mass of IT companies, in his slightly eccentric location. If clients cannot deal with it, they are not the clients he is looking for.

Oli and JailMake Jamie hope to work together on combining robotics and engineering. So far they have done so on a small scale but there's certainly potential for more.

In 10 years from now, anything could be possible. Physically, Oli said, they really could be anywhere. He'd also like to have made Tableflip a cooperative hub providing a series of services to the community: **"Things matter to us and each person matters."**

Where to next? Within the building, to Caren of Hartley Cycles and also to Genevieve and Merlin at the General Store back in Bellenden Road.

HARTLEY CYCLES

Caren of Hartley Cycles

We met Caren at the shared workshop she rents from Jamie of JailMake. She was filing an elegant frame of a bicycle held in a vice, her current bespoke project.

Hartley Cycles is a young business. Caren set up here a year ago. She lives on a boat in Hackney, and her work here is her first experience of Peckham. Caren trained at the RCA in sculpture and jewellery-making, crafting jewellery before bicycles. It was the metalwork element and her love of cycling that drew her to this business. Many of the tools Caren uses now are from her jewellery-making days, particularly the files.

Caren specialises in bikes for the smaller end of the market, for people who are 5ft4 to 5ft6. Her clients are both men and women, but relative to the overall market, she has more female clients.

Caren can work on a bespoke frame and forks for several months. Component parts are then bought in to complete the bicycle. Caren describes her work as slow and she expects to speed up with experience, but her work will always be a labour of love, a craft. We were struck by the order and beauty of the tools in this workshop.

In 10 years Caren would like to be fully set up with all the tools she requires. She is still investing in these. She would like to go on making handcrafted bespoke bikes, but also to produce made-to-order frames, perhaps even with some staff.

Where to next? Just few steps across the shared workshop to Jake of Rusby Cycles.

RUSBY CYCLES

Jake of Rusby Cycles

Caren has a lot in common with Jake of Rusby Cycles. They each make bespoke cycles from their shared workshop. Their tools mirror each other's, and Jake too was working carefully on one frame, his being a high-end steel frame for a client in Singapore.

Jake has been making Rusby Cycles for four years and selling for three. He trained in sculpture in Scotland. When we asked if he still worked as a sculptor, he looked at his frame; of course, the cycle frames themselves are works of art.

Rusby Cycles are made from high-quality steel tube, which is very thin and light. Jake explains that the whole process of commissioning and completing a bike takes between three and six months. His bikes are generally geared road bikes, with the odd fixed-gear. The process is detailed, with a lot of consulting with clients.

Jake has been in south London since moving down from Scotland five years ago. He has had workshops in Borough and Camberwell, moving on as landlords developed their properties. Here, he rents from Jamie of JailMake.

There's a real sense of communality in these workshops. Each time we popped in at lunchtime everyone was sitting down together to eat. Jake showed us an app Oli from Tableflip had designed to manage their daily lunch rota.

In 10 years Jake would like to be on a yacht somewhere, but if on land, his plan is definitely not to be in London. Perhaps he'd also be doing freelance work installing art shows, as he does now to supplement his income.

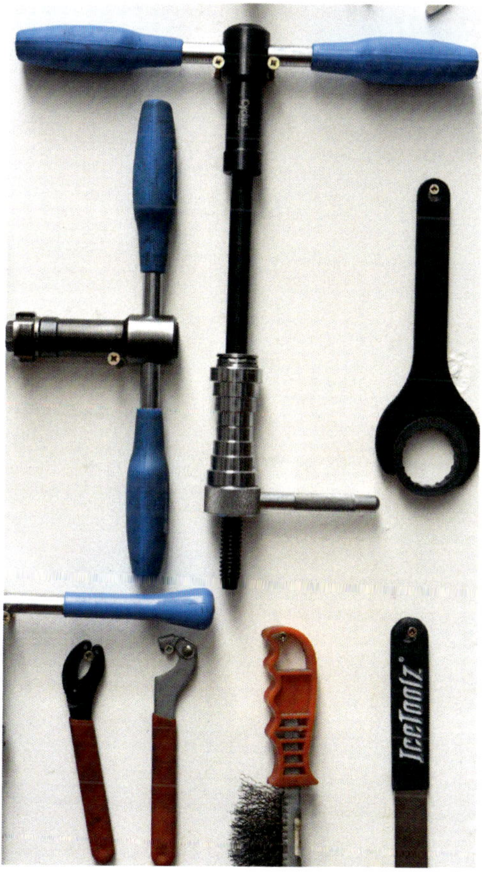

Where to next? Pete of Rat Race Cycles who makes the wheels to order for Rusby Cycles.

R A T
R A C E
C Y C L E S

Team Pete at Rat Race

We were sent to Rat Race Cycles, where Pete and his team, Joel and Dan, were all busy working on cycles in their shop-fronted workshop. They showed us wheels ready to be delivered to Rusby and Hartley Cycles, for frames made by Jake and Caren, soon to be heading to an international bicycle design fair.

Pete, the owner of Rat Race, set up in December 2012. He had planned to open on East Dulwich Grove but was pipped to the post by another independent bike shop. Pete has worked in the bike industry for more than 10 years after completing a degree in physiology, and sees parallels between building bikes and the mechanics of the body. He worked for larger companies to begin with, then set up his own mobile bike-servicing business. Pete is a member of Dulwich Paragon, the second-biggest cycling club in the UK.

The shop's main income comes from servicing and repairing bikes. There's not much money in selling equipment, because people buy online and margins are small. But Pete also specialises in making wheels, which he describes as **"a spin-off business"**. We discussed how bike shops, both old and new, are increasingly starting to work together: Pete, for example, meets up regularly with people from Brixton Cycles and the long-established Edwardes of Camberwell.

Pete would like still to be here in 10 years but for the shop to be bigger - not a chain, but one shop with a great reputation.

And where to next? Across the road to Bambuni, the first of a new wave of shops in the area. The owner had tipped off Pete on the availability of his shop's premises.

BAMBUNI

Huey of Bambuni

Huey showed a keen interest in The Peckham Connection, having lived in Peckham for 15 years. He knew the majority of the businesses we had visited so far.

Huey was working as a carpenter when he spotted the Bambuni building for sale. He took it on as a development project and the delicatessen followed. The interior fittings and furnishing are a tribute to Huey's hard work – he made up the name Bambuni because of his obsession with bamboo.

Huey's dream had been to set up a specialist cheese and wine shop. But it had not taken long for the shop to diversify, becoming a delicatessen with a coffee shop/café and licence to sell alcohol. One hundred and fifty different suppliers now deliver to the shop, bringing cheeses, wines, craft beers, charcuterie, dried foods, oils, bread, pastries and condiments. Huey had expected customers to have a coffee, eat and shop, but in reality this crossover is small. Huey's challenge is to increase footfall in his shop, possibly by narrowing his range through specialisation. There are now six part-time staff at Bambuni, valued as Huey believes that a good team is essential to running any small business.

As we were leaving, Jesse, Huey's one-year-old son, arrived with his mother. He's a known and happy member of the team, and the reason Bambuni doesn't open late at the moment. Huey is currently immersing himself in the business of being a father, which he can do because he's his own boss.

In 10 years, Huey was not sure where he would be. His first thought was that he would be the father to an 11-year-old, which seemed a long way off.

Where to next? To Tom at Gosnells in Print Village , which brews mead. Perfect for this project, as Jackie from Quick Print had told us that Peckham was known as Print Village in the past.

G O S N E L L S

Mead makers

Gosnells' mead is brewed in a unit in Print Village, an industrial unit off Chadwick Road. Tom Gosnell moved here from Walthamstow when a larger distillery he had used closed down. He now employs two full-time workers, plus James, who helps with brewing as well as publicity and marketing. Tom previously worked as a corporate strategist at Virgin Media – great experience for growing a business of his own.

The unit was buzzing with a real sense of growth and ambition. Tom wants mead to become a real contender in the growing craft-beer sector. Gosnells is one of only a handful of mead makers in the UK and specialises in mead with a modern twist, lighter than more traditional brews.

The kit in the brewery is like a scene from Breaking Bad, except that the key ingredient is honey. Gosnells uses Spanish orange-blossom honey, chosen for its flavour and its consistency. They'd like to experiment with local honeys for limited-edition batches in the future, but as a young brewery they want a consistent flavour for the brand. On the day we were there a quarter of a tonne of honey was being poured into vats to start a new batch and 3,000 bottles had just been labelled, ready to go. The boys were busy. Everything was made and carried out by hand.

A designer friend helped out with the branding, which is bee-themed, simply yet beautifully styled. We loved the beeswaxed table, the honey-barrel lights and the bottle labels.

In 10 years Tom would like to be working for a greatly expanded Gosnells, and for mead to have become a drink of choice across the UK.

Where to next?

We were sent to Lerryn’s restaurant, but we already had our 50 before we got there.

GENERAL STORE

Genevieve and Merlin's store

The General Store is owned by a husband-and-wife team who set up their own business as a means to spending time together. Their relationship of 10 years was for many years a long-distance one, even transatlantic, with Genevieve being American.

Genevieve and Merlin met as students at the University of East Anglia, she of poetry and creative writing and he of politics. Thinking of a way of working together, they kept returning to their common interest in food. So they set off independently to train, living apart while putting together a business plan, Merlin taking up an apprenticeship in cheese-making and Genevieve as a baker.

It was clear to them that they would not be able to afford to buy into the property market in London. Living in North London and visiting SE15 they chanced upon their building. It was available to rent and had living accommodation above. They took the risk and two years later are living a simple life at the beautiful General Store, selling foods from small-scale and sustainable producers.

Genevieve and Merlin have an old-fashioned model of work with low overheads. They live and work together with no additional staff, which means that when they take a holiday, the shop closes.

The greatest challenge to small businesses is being the victim of their own success. When we visited, Genevieve and Merlin's landlord had just announced a rent review based on how well their shop had been doing.

Merlin and Genevieve's view is that they hope to be in Peckham for many years, but are aware that they are part of a bigger cycle of change. They showed us old pictures they had been given, showing their shop in several previous guises, including as an aquatic supplies shop.

Where to next?

Ali Baba Juice, which is run by Chris and Sienna another transatlantic pair.

ALI BABA JUICE

Chris & Sienna's juice bar

Ali Baba Juice is in an alley behind a fruit stall on Rye Lane. We met Chris and Sienna at their stall on a cold rainy day and were struck by their energy and hardiness. Though apparently, the weather was not a patch on what they had on their opening weekend, which was during a hurricane.

Being in Peckham, we were told, was a total accident, although they had been living in the area for 10 years. They both have an arts and media background and had had a pilot for a children's TV programme put on hold. They needed to be busy and all the produce in Peckham inspired them: **"We could juice the whole area."**

Early experiments were with puna yams, sold everywhere locally. Chris and Sienna have a passion for creating flavours using the produce surrounding them, making affordable juices. The current most popular juice is apple, kale and basil. There are some classics on the menu but they are always experimenting with new flavours.

We spoke for 15 minutes and in that time they served a stream of customers, all known to them. Chris and Sienna share a real sense of belonging and loving being here. On being asked about the next 10 years they are determined that they will still be here. They say that they have no plan to franchise – it's not that kind of project.

The juice stall is core to many exciting developments. They already run Ali Baba's Cocktail bar behind the Bussey Building on Friday and Saturday nights, and bottle cold-pressed Ali Baba Juices, which they sell at their bar, and in a few local retail outlets and cafés. And there's more to come, including talk of a milk float. Their enthusiasm is contagious and their energy boundless.

Where to next? Jahson at Zionly Arts in Rye Lane Market. And to Hassan, their mentor and neighbour on Ali's Veg Stall.

ALI'S VEG STALL

Hassan the man

Hassan's vegetable stall is named after his brother, Ali, who died in his thirties. Hassan and his family fled from Iraqi Kurdistan more than 30 years ago and have now established a growing web of enterprise in Peckham. He is also landlord to Ali Baba's Juice next door.

Hassan's first work was as a van driver. In the early 1980s he started at a fruit'n'veg stall opposite where he is now. Then the man who owned his current pitch died and Hassan took on the pitch – a shrewd move when Peckham was cheap. He remembers taking £200 on his first day. Hassan lives in south-west London, where it is too expensive for him to set up.

Hassan is proud of his business brain. He moves and develops with the times. He has a canary in a cage by his stall. He likes his birds but also notices how they attract his customers, making them more likely to return. Hassan is a specialist. Jamaicans are his preferred customers and so he carefully caters for them. Hassan is proud of the freshness of his stock. Rather than offering three for a pound as other stalls do, he sells in small quantities, with yams cut to the right weight for a soup or a stew. This encourages customers to return regularly and to buy extras on each visit, and what they buy is always very fresh. Hassan understands that this is what his customers want.

Hassan sent us on to Yada's, his new business initiative, a restaurant that aims to tap into the influx of young hipsters of Peckham. Yada's was still setting up when we visited, it opened briefly over the summer but closed again. Hassan has ambitious plans for Yada's, including a late-opening hookah lounge.

Hassan would like to be retired in 10 years', travelling and going on holiday. He hopes his businesses, reputation and legacy will continue beyond his retirement.

HURRICANE HITS ENGLAND
THE CANON
ATLANTIS
HERMETIC MYSTERY
THE SERPENT POWER

ZIONLY ARTS

Jahson's emporium

Sienna and Chris sent us to Jahson as he was someone they had sought inspiration from for many years. They were influenced by his aesthetic and benefitted from his wisdom. Jahson owns Zionly Art Gallery in Rye Lane Market. He describes himself as a philanthropic businessman.

Jahson added the H to his name, to add a Rasta twist. He was born in Brixton where he lived until he was three, then spent a few years in Jamaica. Then when he was eight he returned to London to live on the North Peckham Estate. He has been in Rye Lane Market for five years.

Jahson is a busy entrepreneur: everything, he says, is linked by conscious thought, nothing is random. He describes himself as an ergonomic thinker. He was raised not to work for anyone and he is a man of many trades, restauranteur, electrician, trader and mechanic. Jahson is full of positive energy and very much alive, thriving on very little sleep.

Books,artwork,fabrics,musical instruments and alternative medicines surround Jahson, all Africa-centred as he explains, though he also sells Caribbean and British materials. The shop is well stocked but not in the least bit chaotic. Jahson is also a consultant on life and health to many; he is there to talk and listen to his customers. He moved from Brixton Market because of soaring rents and a changing market - Peckham, he says, is more raw and real, like Brixton used to be. Jahson's ethos is that everything is attainable with hard work. Whenever he has expanded it has been through self-financing. He next wants to open a vegan restaurant.

In 10 years Jahson would like to run a three-storey department store, ideally on the site of the old Jones and Higgins on Peckham Rye. It would be a one-stop shop full of African styling.

Where to next?

To Michael de Souza, whose shop had just opened next door in the market, as part of Jahson's bigger plan to promote Rastamouse.

RASTAMOUSE

Michael de Souza's Rastamouse

Jahson sent us next door but one to the new shop aptly named All Tings Rastamouse. Here were we met Michael de Souza, the creator and writer of Rastamouse, who has found a good new home in Peckham. Michael, new to the area, lives in Notting Hill.

Michael's passion is for writing and, through this, opening up the world of literacy to young children in an exciting and relevant way. Rastamouse is a simple story, written in rhyme, about a young black mouse living on his wits. **"Through love and respect Rastamouse will always make a bad ting good!"** Rastamouse poems, which have been published in books, televised and recorded as songs and rap, make a good platform to engage with young black children, who are under-represented in literature. Michael is enthusiastic, energetic and influential. Last week he was a panel judge for Blue Peter's fiction and non-fiction book prize.

Before Rastamouse, Michael was a swimming instructor, singing and dancing as Professor Splash to eradicate children's fear of water. At the same time he made up poems for his own kids. He teamed up with Genevieve, a friend and publicist, and Rastamouse was created. They self-published their first book in 2003 and Michael went hot-footing around shops.

Rastamouse took off, becoming a hit on CBeebies, Michael went to Cannes, and Lenny Henry read the stories on Junior Jackanory. In spite of this success there was resistance from buyers. No one was stocking Rastamouse merchandise. This is where Jahson stepped in, aiming to make Rastamouse more widely available.

In 10 years Michael would like to be retired and for Rastamouse to be a legacy.

Where to next?

Michael directed us to Ricardo at the gaming store opposite.

R M GAMES

Ricardo plays games

Michael from Rastamouse sent us to Ricardo opposite, who sells new and second-hand computer games and consoles, mainly for X-Box and PlayStation.

R M Games is one of the oldest businesses in the market. Ricardo set it up 13 years ago, when he was just 18 years old. Ricardo, who grew up in Peckham, left Warwick Park School (now Peckham Academy) when he was 16 and started work in Game, one of the biggest retailers of computer games, where he excelled.

After a couple of years at Game, Ricardo wanted to be his own boss and felt he could do what he was doing there for himself. It was hard at first, he said, very different from working for a big company. To buy his first stock he had to sell his car. He wonders whether he would have been so fearless if he had had more knowledge.

By 2006-2007 he had two or three people working with him. But now he has reduced his overheads and works alone, six days a week, from 10am until 5.30pm. He also works part-time for a cab firm in Peckham and so is really working 24/7.

Ricardo's customers are mostly local and regular. We were amused to hear that Ricardo hopes to keep his young son away from consoles as long as possible.

In 10 years Ricardo would like to be on a sunny island, making up for the many non-daylight hours he has spent in the covered market. He can also see himself as a full-time cab driver.

Where to next? That was easy, to Jenny's near Peckham Rye station. Ricardo has been eating there for years, and says the customer service is exceptional and friendly.

JENNY'S

Seyit of Jenny's

Ricardo from R M Games sent us to Jenny's, his local café. We could see that this was a place with many regulars, and the feel of a 1980s diner. Jenny's is a large café with 78 seats and five staff, including Seyit, the manager, just a few steps away from Peckham Rye station, now a focus for redevelopment.

The first Jenny's was set up more than 20 years ago as a franchise, later bought out by its owner. It has catered for generations of families in Peckham. Inside was busy and the atmosphere friendly; half the custom is local and regular, and the station also brings in commuting trade, and enables Seyit to commute to work very easily from north London. The best-seller is the all-day breakfast. The menu, however, is diverse, embracing elements of Turkish food, a falafel wrap being the most recent addition.

Seyit has been working here for 10 years and has seen much change in Peckham. The area has become busier, with many more people out on the pavements, making it feel safer.

Where would Seyit like to be in 10 years?
"Still going like this. I am happy like this."
But a conversation as we were leaving highlighted the vulnerability of Jenny's, with the proposed regeneration of Peckham Rye Station. The new plans will not offer a space of this size, and therefore of this type of café.

Where to next? To Elaine, who runs a card stall, in front of the cinema. Seyit chose her as an active supporter of the business community in face of the many changes that are afoot.

ELAINE'S CARDS

Greetings from Elaine

Elaine has been running the card stall on the pavement in front of the PeckhamPlex cinema for more than 30 years. We found her there with her mum and dad, who often help out, as well as Jason, a part-time assistant, who has worked on the stall since leaving school six years ago.

Elaine's stall doesn't just sell cards. She also has clothes, including T-shirts, underwear and colourful summer dresses. When she started her business in 1984 she specialised in over-sized ladieswear. Over the years, though, she has gradually moved into greetings cards, as they have turned out to be the main moneymaker. Other stock changes throughout the year; in spring it's mostly hats; in winter, it could be umbrellas.

Elaine set up her own stall because she did not want to work for anyone, and had distant family members already running a fruit 'n' veg stall. She has seen many changes in Peckham and is both a proactive member of various trade associations and an active campaigner for the business community. Now, she's fighting the current wave of development. She says she has a positive view of development so long as it incorporates everyone's interests and isn't just aimed at gentrification.

"The fewer words greetings cards have in them, the more expensive they seem to be." The new wave of Peckham locals don't buy cards from her stall because her cards have too may words in them. But Elaine loves that she is now serving mothers with children who started coming to the stall with their mothers when they were young.

In 10 years, Elaine thinks she'll either still be here or she'll have retired.

And where does Elaine think we should go next? She suggests Albert on the luggage stall just across the road, and Barry’s Café next to the station.

ALBERT'S LUGGAGE

Albert's case study

We found Albert having lunch in Jenny's Restaurant, which he generously offered to share with us. It was Election Day 2015, which led to an interesting chat about politics and Albert's involvement with the local Labour Party in Peckham, his home.

Albert started running a market stall around 20 years ago at the junction of Rye Lane and Choumert Road. He was allocated the pitch after attempting to sell designer-copied sunglasses from a table outside what is now Kahn's Bargains. A policeman directed him to Southwark Council for an official pitch; after seven years he moved to his current prime pitch nearer to the station. Albert previously worked in customs offices which were closed down. He woke up the day after and realised he wanted and needed to do something for himself. Today his surroundings have totally changed. The large department stores have gone and there are more stalls and smaller shops.

Albert has two students working with him. On weekdays they can manage without him but on Saturdays he tries always to e there. Albert sells bags including luggage, briefcases, aundry bags and handbags. Albert has a large, strong ustomer base. In the area there are many African, Latino nd others living in London and returning home with large ases of gifts and goods. The suitcases are invariably eft behind and his customers return to him again and gain. Each day Albert packs his stock into his large VW an and takes it to his parking bay five minutes away and hen he walks home.

Where
will
you
be
in
ten
years?

“Not here.”

He will be 68 years old, still in business and, he hopes, living in both Ghana and London.

Albert walked us along Rye Lane to introduce us in person to Hussain at Hax International.

HAX INTERNATIONAL

Hussain of Hax

Hussain, the owner and manager of this store specialising in all things West African in general and Sierra Leonean in particular, has been on Rye Lane for four years. Before that he was round the corner on Choumert Road.

The shop is stocked from floor to ceiling with drums of oil, sacks of rice, refrigerated and dried foods and kitchen equipment. Everything has a West African flavour, and cassava is one of the biggest sellers. There are four staff in the shop, plus other friends and family who pop in to help. Hussain is constantly on the telephone trading, checking prices and making orders. Most stock is sourced from large wholesalers.

Hussain tells us that his customers are mainly from Sierra Leone and Côte d'Ivoire. This has not changed over the years, but recently trade has been slower, with customers spending less money as a result of the recession. The regulars still come, but instead of spending £20 will now spend only £5. Money transfer is an additional service for customers, many of whom send money home to their families on a regular basis.

As we left the shop we spotted Hussain's cousin helping an elderly customer to the bus stop with her shopping.

In 10 years Hussain imagines himself being on a beautiful beach in Sierra Leone or Lebanon; but only for a holiday as he is now settled in London.

Where to next? Ncxt door to the Makeover hair stylists. We were delighted by this choice as we had started our project hoping for the chance to photograph one of Peckham's many salons.

THE MAKEOVER

Styled by Eric

It took us months to track down Eric, the owner of the Makeover hair salon. Then finally Eric was there one day, rearranging the salon furniture. It was worth the wait. Eric greeted us with the most impressive handshake, a skill learnt from the years he had spent working as a butler.

Eric had been keen to run his own business for a long time, and in 2009 a friend approached him about a hair salon. Today he rents out chairs to 10 self-employed stylists, and the salon also has a nail table. Eric's role is to manage the work setting. There are, of course, many hair salons in Peckham, but this is the only one with individual cubicles.

Eric is proud of the comparative calm of his place. It is a community hub, but can also offer privacy and a more relaxing environment if wanted – the ambience is important when customers regularly spend up to nine hours at a time at the salon. This, as well as talented stylists, is why many customers travel from across and even outside London to get their hair done at the Makeover. The salon is officially open from 9am until 9pm, but in reality stays open until midnight if needed.

The Makeover has a mixture of West Indian and African stylists. Customers are likely choose an African stylist for plaits and a West Indian one for twists, although in reality things are more fluid, with African customers choosing Caribbean styles and vice versa, and changing over time. Wig-caps are made by all the stylists using hair from Africa, China, Brazil and England, almost everywhere in the world.

In 10 years Eric would like to be running a second shop in Luton. Eric believes there would be enough local business, and customers would travel for his reputation.

In 10 years Barry would like simply to be alive and well.

Barry refers us to D Peacock & Son, a local garage, with whom he has a long history, he says.

D PEACOCK & SON

Proud Peacocks

We had just arrived at Peacock's to talk to Andrew, when who should turn up but Barry, who had sent us here.

Peacock's is now a third-generation family business. It was set up in 1945 by Denis, Andrew's grandfather, in what used to be the stables for a local dairy. Barry had worked for Denis when he was 17, and, as the youngest of the group, had often got into trouble as their fall guy.

In 1994, the very day after he left school, Andrew started working at the garage. He learned the skills needed, including specialist welding. Sadly, in 2009 Andrew's dad, David, died and he took over running the show. But the reality was hard work in a trade that was becoming tougher. When Peacock's first set up, the bulk of its business was fixing second-hand cars owned by the local community. But now, many neighbourhood residents have expensive new cars on service contracts with dealerships. Improved transport links and the increased popularity of cycling also mean fewer drivers. Also, the engines of modern cars are difficult to access and diagnose.

Paul, who has a long history with the family, was busy at the back of the garage working on body repairs - a skill which is perhaps more transferable to the modern car. And Andrew's mum, Maxine, comes in once week to keep the office and accounts shipshape. His dad moved the family to Sidcup, where Andrew still lives today. He travels to work by train, not by car.

In 10 years Andrew is emphatic that he will still be here in Peckham: he loves the atmosphere and the people. He'd never move his business to Sidcup but he'd love to live in Peckham, and would if he could afford it.

THAMES
GALLERY

Pauline in the frame

Pauline set up the Thames Gallery in 1986. Before that, she and her husband ran an art gallery in Putney, and framing was a branch of this. They chose their building for its large frontage – it had previously been a car showroom. It was clearly a good choice, as they have not needed to move again.

Pauline's daughter Zoe has now joined the family business. She was serving a customer who had brought in several paintings to be framed. The high level of service and her attention to detail was evident. Zoe studied at the RCA and Slade; her mum felt that her training was an asset, not only in her artistry, but also in the practical way she has organised everything. The workshop revealed a lovely large central work-table, with great light, plus neatly organized areas for glass, mounts and frames, as well as the beautiful dog Sparky.

We asked about change more generally and Pauline first spoke of the facelift given to the parade of shops 15 years ago as part of the Bellenden Road regeneration, which included Zandra Rhodes bollards and lamp posts. This did not have a big impact on her business, but improved the area in general.

More specifically to her work, she described changes n the art being brought to the shop. When they started, he majority of their work was framing posters and reproductions. **Now it is more modern, urban and more original works. A lot of people buy art now."** Most of the customers are local, ut some have moved away and still use Thames Gallery. The locals eem to be younger these days, and perhaps more affluent.

In 10 years Pauline hopes to have retired, with her daughter to be running the business in her own way. **"It suits us all."** Zoe can balance her interests in art and business with her young family.

Pauline sent us on to Chris Clack, a local printer. Exciting for us as we've heard a lot about Chris through our photography.

DULWICH PRINTS & PRINTING

Chris Clack the printer

Chris Clack runs Dulwich Prints and Printing from his home. This is a happy referral for us as Chris has been recommended to us for our photography business. Our small worry was that we were straying from SE15 by going to Dulwich Print and Printing. But no, Chris had called his company Dulwich Print when he set up nine years ago, because at that time it had seemed as if it would attract more business than Peckham Prints with that name. We all pondered that this probably was no longer the case.

Chris is a one-man show and his work is full-time. He trained at Camberwell and RCA and continues to work as a practising artist. To begin with he was producing only his own images digitally, using large-format printers, then over the years he started printing for others. In his front room his own work is evident with his bold portraits. Ronnie and Betty, two cherished whippets, are very present in both real life and in print.

Chris's business operates by appointment. People do ring on the door in passing, but he's often not there - he may be walking the dogs or preoccupied with a print job. Chris not only prints but also provides an advisory service to his clients. He is valued as a knowledge base.

When asked where he would like to be in 10 years, he said he'd like to still be doing what he's doing, but part-time. He'd like to be doing more of his own work, ideally combining this with high-quality printing for other artists, work that really reflects his skills. We had a real sense that Chris loves his work.

Where to next? Chris sent us to Mark Francis, a local artist, whose work he is currently printing.

MARK FRANCIS STUDIO

Mark's marks

Chris Clack directed us to Mark Francis at Nutbrook Studios, tucked away just off a residential area. Chris was producing 80 prints in four colours for one of his galleries. We could see the first of these prints Mark had just received.

It was a treat for us to be sent to Mark, who has the added connection of being a friend. For us, then, his studio was easy to find. In Victorian times the site was a laundry and then became one of the many printers in the area, as mentioned by Jackie at Quick Print. Mark heard of the property from friends living on the street, and moved his studio here four years ago. He loves it.

Mark's studio has been tailor-made and as a result has the perfect ambience for him, a bespoke studio. And, as importantly, it's close to home, just a 10-minute walk. Mark's partner, also an artist, is in the studio above. Each day Mark travels back and forth from work, often having lunch at home and always starting work after walking Bella, his dog, often crossing paths with Chris and his whippets.

In the studio Mark was priming a canvas for a new work, surrounded by his paintings, and sculptures too. We were shown his most recent pieces, which he described as rougher and grittier than his previous work. He is playing with the varnishes and glazes, examining the archaeology of the painting. These new works had evolved since a residency with the London Mathematical Society, as a part of its 150th-anniversary celebrations. Yesterday a group of mathematicians visited his studio and Mark has been attending mathematical lectures to stimulate ideas and creativity.

In 10 years Mark would still like to be here in his studio. In fact he would like to be here until the day he dies, as he never intends to retire. This could well be a reality for Mark, who has the added security of part-owning the building.

Where to next?

Mark directed us to Lou at Captured on the Rye.

CAPTURED ON THE RYE

Lou captured

We met Lou where he is happiest, beavering away in his studio under the arches off Blenheim Grove. Contorted dried frogs surrounded him. He has collected them from his garden and is planning to electroplate them with copper and silver. We were as excited by this as Lou was, and returned a couple of weeks later to check in on the success of his frog project.

Lou's designs are taken from nature, with an added Peckham twist, the crows (corvus) of Peckham Rye being one of his first and strongest Made in Peckham images. His more recent frog design has not been such a big seller. And customers don't like the wasp, but Lou likes that it has a bit of edge, rather than the friendly bee.

Lou's background is in art and as a maker of things. He is a photographer, designer and printer and set up Captured on the Rye six years ago. He has also more recently opened a shop in East Dulwich as an outlet for his work. But he does not like to play shopkeeper, and is much more at home in his studio. He also makes rock music videos, and would like to build on this side of his creativity.

Another business strand is kids' parties. Lou offers screen-printed T-shirt parties and spin-painting parties. These make steady money and support his other enterprises. The plan is that Lou will soon step back and employ others to host the parties.

In 10 years Lou says he will still be producing Made in Peckham, but perhaps from the Kent coast.

Where to next?

Lou suggested Blenheim Forge, the young knife-makers next door. A good send, as we had previously been sent to the same unit to meet Andy the metalworker, who had moved on.

BLENHEIM FORGE

The knife boys

Lou from Captured in the Rye sent us to James and Jon, who had become knife-makers through experimenting with Andy's steel foundry and tools.

We were mesmerised by the smoke, heat and noise of this small foundry: it was like stepping back in time. The raw materials and tools used by Blenheim Forge are enduring. But, as we learned, James and Jon are people with a love of craftsmanship and precision. These friends make hand-forged knives and they love it so much that they work whenever they can, often seven days a week. Rich has recently joined the team, mainly making tools for them. He is currently working on a York-stone grinding wheel.

This is a specialist trade. Only a handful of businesses make hand-forged knives across the whole UK. James, a design engineer, and Jon, a philosophy scholar, started out messing around on a hand-built forge, in their garden at first and later on at Andy's forge on Sundays. One day they watched a YouTube clip on knife-making and how to make Damascus steel. They had a go and were successful first time.

We saw James and Jon making a knife for Charlie at Flock & Herd, the local butcher. This seems to be a great marketing opportunity. They were also making a specialist BBQ for a Jamie Oliver restaurant and a knife for Nigella Lawson. But it is clear that creating is their first love.

In 10 years James and Jon hope they will still be making knives together. Perhaps they will become quicker with experience, but they say they'll never become automated.

Where to next?

Tom the Etcher, who shares their workspace.

TOM'S ETCHING STUDIO

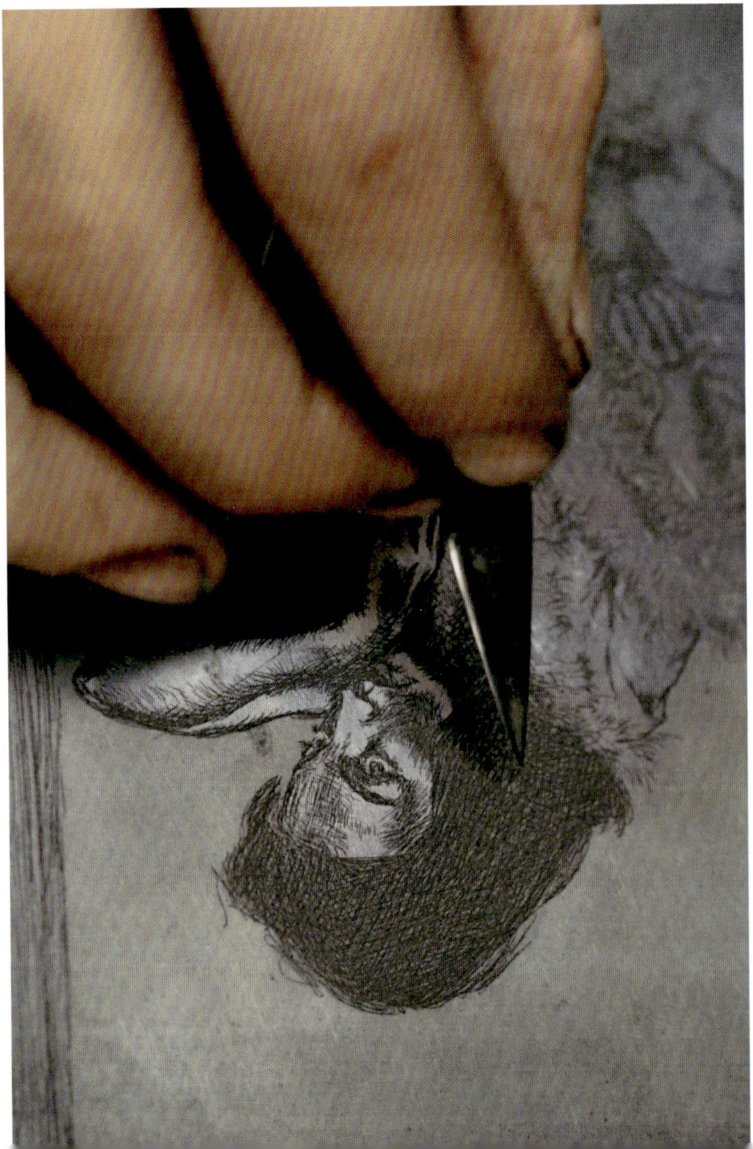

Sketching and etching

Tom shares an arch with Blenheim Forge. Before that, he worked from a shed in the garden of the house he used to share with his friend James. Tom now lives in Nunhead and cycles the short distance to work.

When the arch became available, James and Tom saw it as a business opportunity, and Tom's work responded to the space he had. He set about making himself a large steel press, now a key feature of his workplace. There aren't many etching studio spaces available because of the costs of the printing press. Artists pay Tom to use his studio space. This helps Tom financially but does not distract him from his own work,

Tom studied fine art at Central Saint Martins. We looked through his latest works, which had a very definite Peckham theme. It was a treat for us to recognise places and faces we had encountered through working on The Peckham Connection.

In 10 years Tom would like to be selling his works: perhaps here, perhaps in South America.

Where to next? Tom sent us to a new gallery space very recently opened, Bosse & Baum. We had already reached our 50th business and so ended here. But we did go there the next day to see Congregation, a fantastic exhibition on local churches in unlikely places.

R O Y A
TEXTILE

Thank you Mo

We passed Roya Textile many times in our journeys up and down Peckham Rye. It sells a huge and beautifully displayed range of African print fabrics, neatly stacked in six-yard bundles, which greatly appealed to us. The shop is tidy, bright, and irresistible.

Mo, who was covering for his father, was happy to be included in our project. Mo's other job is manufacturing industrial doors, which he said is more technical but not as fun as working at Roya. He likes both! Mo's family was from Afghanistan. His father set this business up four years ago in a smaller shop along the Rye, and before that, had a fabric shop for two years in Brixton. He moved to Peckham for the market, because his main custom comes from people and traders with connections with West Africa.

The shop represents the history of African textiles. A small percentage of the fabrics are made in Africa but most are Dutch, reflecting colonial trade relations, and increasingly many are produced in China and India. One Nigerian customer explained that she buys fabric in Peckham to take with her to Nigeria to be tailored. It wasn't that she couldn't buy the same things in Nigeria, but this way was simple for her and less time-consuming.

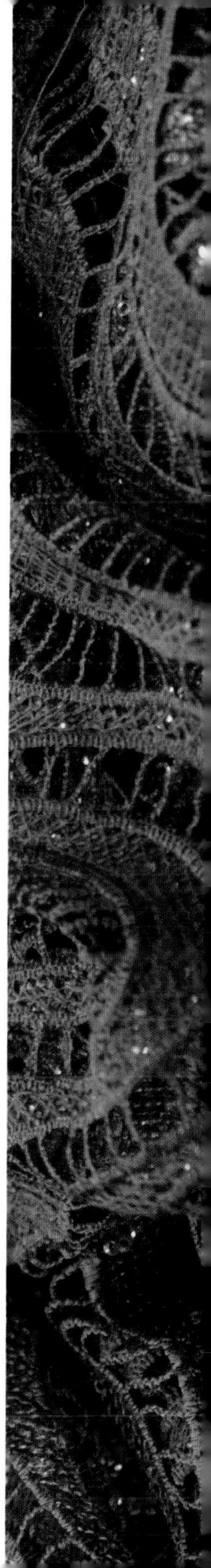

Around 60 per cent of Roya's trade is retail and the remaining business is wholesale. The retail is often passing trade – someone might be attracted in by the fabrics and end up buying six yards to make an outfit. Or it could also be a bulk purchase for an event. For a wedding, the bride and groom choose a fabric and then may request 100 or more outfits to be made of one print. Choosing often takes several hours, with the unraveling of many bundles. People visit the shop from right across London.

Where would you like to be in 10 years?
Doing the same business, but in a bigger shop, on a busier section of Rye Lane.

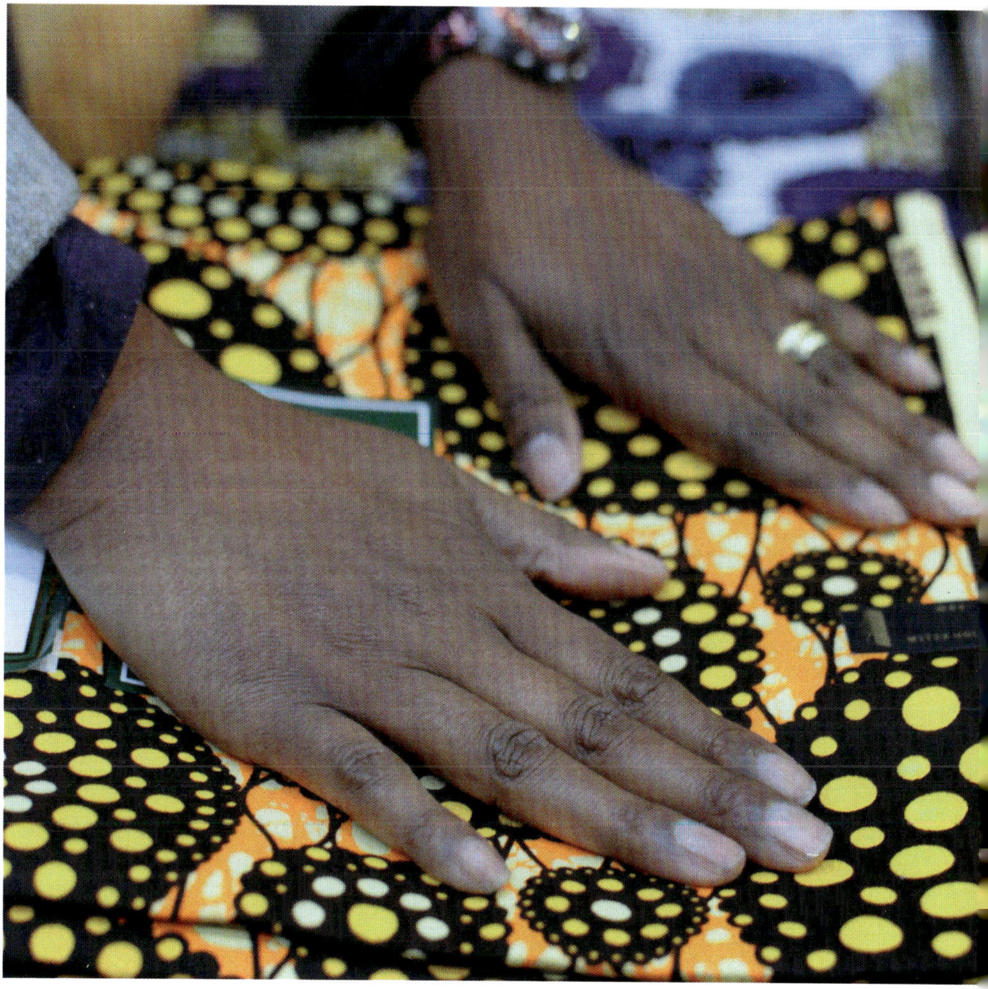

This, our 50th business,
marks the end of The Peckham Connection.

ACKNOWLEDGEMENTS

We would like to thank all the people who took part in this project and who gave us all our connections.

Ezra-Lloyd Jackson of DVLOP for his design.

Janette Parris for allowing us to use her amazing artwork from Peckham Promenade on the cover.

Keith Turpin for writing a picturesque Peckham preface.

And the valuable support, advice and encouragement from

Ginette Casey **Nicky Hirst**
Rachel Baker **Jenny Turner**
Jane Langley and Blue Patch
Sue Hill **Veronica Simpson** **Clare Price**
Kate White at Peckham Peculiar **Michael Carter**
Julia Honess **Clare Dowdy**

XOXOXOXOXOXOXOXOXOXOXOXOXOXOXOXOXOXO

And to everyone who Kickstarter pledges have enabled u to make the Peckham Connection a reality.

In the Right Light will donate £1 from the sale of eac book to Rye Lane Traders' Association.

XOXO
“Invisible threads
are the strongest ties”
Friedrich Nietzsche